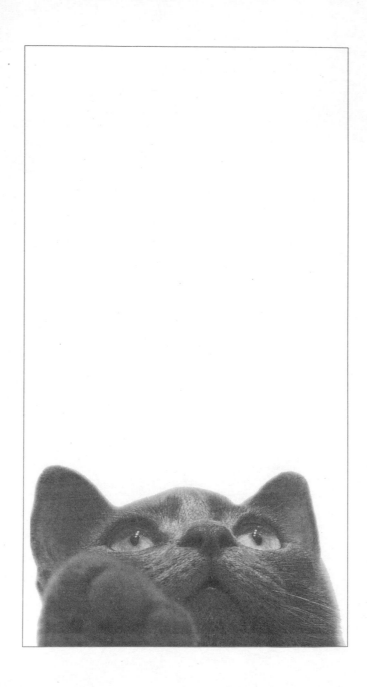

THE PHILOSOPHY
OF CATS

THE
PHILOSOPHY
OF CATS

by

Federica Sgarbi

GIBSON SQUARE

To Kiwi and Little Dove,
Pearl and Pinocchio.

First edition published by Gibson Square Books

www.gibsonsquare.com

ISBN: 9781908096036

Printed and bound by CPI Group (UK) Ltd, Croydon, CR0 4YY

'If ... a scientific civilisation is to be a good civilisation it is necessary that increase in knowledge should be accompanied by increase in wisdom.'

Bertrand Russell, *The Scientific Outlook*

Contents

Purrface 13
The Philosophy of Cats 15
The Cats
    Bottoms Up 23
    Sovereign 31
    Ying Yang 39
    Itty-Bitty 45
    Jerry 49
    Mowgli 55
    Tabby 59
    Gorgeous 63
    Spitfire 69
    Swami 75
    Cats and Newspapers 79
    Blessed and Santiago 91
    Little Dove 95

Appendices
Cats and Names 103
Garfield and Pin Pin 107
Cats and Poets 119
Pawsabilities for Cat Rescuers 125

Purrface

If you have bought, or are about to buy, this book, it's probably because you love the quietness of the moon, herbal teas in decorated ceramic mugs, the light of a candle, the flowing of its wax, the smell of printed paper and – obviously – cats.

If you love these things, you are certainly a positive person. And if this is true, you'll love the added sweetness that reading a bit of philosophy can bring to everyday experiences.

Now, know that the stories you are about to read are true. But before the cats can make their entrance, I have to explain how everything began...

The Philosophy of Cats

If on a Saturday or Sunday morning you don't know what to do, go and visit a cattery (or a kennel) in your town. You might think, 'No, I can't. If I go there, I will feel guilty... Those cats, poor things, I'd want to bring them all home with me!' And feeling this way, you'd probably decide to stay home.

I, too, wasn't in a position to adopt all the cattery's guests – all the kittens found in the countryside or the ones abandoned in the street because of the summer holidays. At the time I was living in the centre of town, in a flat where two cats, Pearl and Pinocchio, already reigned supreme.

Therefore, when I decided to go to the cattery one Saturday afternoon, I went even though I knew that I couldn't have any more cats than the ones I had. But sometimes ideas are irrepressible, so I thought it better to go anyway.

The building was picturesque: tall trees in the garden and a big cat muzzle painted on the bell. But the incinerator in the background, the cages, the meows and the smell of pee made me hesitate for an instant whether to go through with my visit.

The guests numbered seventy-eight, of every age, of every colour and of every character. Cats are proud animals and are most in their element when seated on the garden wall or asleep on the sofa. To see them in cages tugged at my conscience. There wasn't, however, anything I could do. I couldn't even adopt one, let alone all seventy-eight of them. And, anyway, many more would continue to arrive.

How many cats have been important in your life? Have you ever thought about it? The one that belonged to your parents or grandparents, the one adopted when you first went to live by yourself, the one that came to see you at the house rented by the seaside or in the mountains because you gave him a bit of milk... The tabby, the black and white one, the Persian, the Siamese... They are all linked to a memory of agreeable company. As Stuart MacMillan used to say, 'a meow massages the heart.'

I can't deny that, in that context, the meows I heard coming from the rooms and cages were rather upsetting. It was as if it was impossible for these cats to express the 'catness' that I so passionately love. But then again, there was nothing I could do.

Yet, these poor seventy-eight cats shorn of their true nature kept crossing my mind and I wanted to do something for them. But what?

I talked to relatives and friends, and someone even told me that philosophers like me (well, I have a doctorate in philosophy) do not possess much common sense: everybody knows that philosophy is impractical and detached from reality...

On the contrary, it was exactly by meditating on the situation, reflecting in peace, that I came upon the simplest way to solve it. I knew that there are a lot of generous, understanding people who, like you and me, love cats. I would let them know about the cattery's guests and the problem would solve itself.

I began a long filing process, entering the data of all of seventy-eight cats present in the cattery. For each one of them we had to know age, health, personality, and any individual anecdotes.

Moreover, it was important, I thought, to give each one of them the name that best suited him or her. I couldn't call a shy, one-kilo cat 'Lion,' nor could I call a big, nine-kilo guy 'Feather.'

I created a table that summarised each cat's information and, after carefully thinking about their story, I assigned each one a name that said something about their background and character. Next, I discussed my plan with the cattery's director. Every day, I would write adverts to be published in the local newspapers in which I would introduce, little by little, all the guests of the organisation. She agreed, as long as I committed to managing it all by myself. A colleague of hers was much less willing. As far as she was concerned, I was only burdening her with lots of new names to remember.

But once the director agreed, I contacted the newspapers in town; all of them were willing to help, more or less. The seventy-eight cats and I owe them everything because they were vital in spreading the news, and hence, to the adoptions.

Finally, I had to write the truthful and sympathetic adverts to introduce 'my' cats not only to our town but also to the whole area around it. Maybe, in this way I hoped, I could finally give them a home.

The Cats

Bottoms Up

To me, one of the pleasures of a cat's company is his devotion to comfort.
Compton Mackenzie)

One of the first cats I wrote an advert for was Bottoms Up.

He was a classic red tabby, about five years old. He had been named by a lady who looked after the cat colony he came from. Taken to the cattery in order to receive medical treatment for a cold, he had been unable to get well enough to leave again.

Bottoms Up loved comfort. I always found him leaning, seated or lying on some shelf. I discovered afterwards that this wasn't only for comfort's sake – he was depressed and, because of this, he was losing his hair. What's more, his cold became chronic. Used as he was to open spaces, he couldn't get used to the cattery and the garden net that kept the cats inside. Seeing him like that broke my heart. Still and with dull eyes, he was perhaps more a memory of a cat than a real and proper cat. But he still loved cuddles very much. As soon as someone appeared at the door, he dragged himself towards them with a 'meow.' One pat and he cheered up.

Due to his endless capacity for love, he was one of the first cats I described in an advert. At the beginning, still having no style or journalistic experience, I just gave the cat's data. So when I wrote about Bottoms Up the ad only mentioned:

Bottoms Up, male cat, red tabby, five years old, sterilised and vaccinated, sweet and nice, depressed and not in the best of shape, is urgently looking for a home.

Apart from the cattery's address and telephone number, I also put my mobile phone number in the advert. Only afterwards did I realise just how good an idea this was. Aside from Bottoms Up, five other cats were featured in the ad. I received a lot of phone calls for them and, finally, one for Bottoms Up arrived on my mobile. It was morning and I had gone to the cattery to be by the phone, hoping that a crowd had been drawn there by my advert. Thankfully people, and phone calls, came in great numbers.

The lady who rang me on my mobile told me that she wanted some information about Bottoms Up. 'You know, I was looking for a red cat; I already have two others.' I told her that he was fantastic but that he didn't look to be in tip-top shape. She said: 'I don't mean to impose, but you seem so kind. Would you bring him to me?' I told her that was no problem – I had a car – but that she had to take into careful considera-tion that our cat was in somewhat of a delicate condition. She told me that she would have him anyway.

When I went inside to pick him up, Bottoms Up was lying on his side and looking out of a small window. I was so happy to take him away from there that I hadn't considered there might be hiccups on the way!

The cat had a cold and was on medication, so it was necessary for the vet to give the all clear for the adoption. I wasn't aware of this, though, and had already made an appointment with the lady who wanted him. I didn't want to cancel. The appointment was in an hour and I decided to give the vet a call, asking him about Bottoms Up's health and whether it was possible to put him up for adoption. 'Yes, I visited him this morning, and he can be adopted.' I was so relieved.

It was the most wonderful feeling to take Bottoms Up, so trustful, in my arms and think: 'You are going home.' I don't know if he understood, but he started purring. I put him in one of the cattery's carriers and placed it on the car seat next to me. Another problem was that the cattery was at the town's outskirts while the possible adopter lived in the centre, and I had first to go the opposite direction to buy Bottoms Up's drugs. Half of them weren't available when I arrived at the shop. I remembered a second store where I might find the missing ones. I went there as quickly as I could and, during the journey, I kept an eye on him. He was looking around, looking at me, stimulated by all the movement. It was cold, but I had warmed the car and turned on the radio. Bottoms Up was starting to react. Finally, I found all the medicine that he needed.

I arrived at the lady's house almost on time and rang the buzzer saying: 'It's the Cat Girl.' The lady lived on a delightful and extremely narrow street paved with stones that had been worn smooth by people's steps. I opened a small gate and found myself in a spacious and well-kept garden with a beautiful lawn. I lifted the carrier to allow Bottoms Up's big, green eyes to see his new house. The woman let me in. She lived on the ground floor in an apartment perfect for cats, full of wooden beams and shelves to climb on. I put the carrier on the floor and, slowly, opened it. The cat who came out wasn't the Bottoms Up of the cattery. It was a new cat, much younger, agile, curious, who began smelling everything and jumping everywhere. The sick Bottoms Up had remained on the old armchair in the cattery.

I explained to the lady that it was probably better to take it slow, given that she had two other cats. But it was clear that she was able to manage and, after a little chat, I went away. When I left the house Bottoms Up was lying on the bed, a picture of catness.

🐈

I promised that I would complement the events in this book with a bit of philosophy, because it has contributed, in part, to the realisation of this project. So, I am keeping my word.

At the end of each story, you'll find a small

philosophical nugget that seems to me to reflect the personality or the antics of the starring cat. At the beginning of the book, you already had a taste of philosophy: a quotation from Bertrand Russell. He had such an interesting mind, stinging and sharp like all (or almost all) the English. I recommend him. I really enjoyed *The Pursuit of Happiness* but the piece with which I want to reflect upon the first feline adventure in this book is not by him, it's by Kant.

I have often heard people say that he is very difficult to understand. Well, he is complex and you need to be willing to follow him in his 'roundabout way of thinking.' In *Answer to the Question: What is Enlightenment?* for example, you can find his admonishment to eliminate the idea of 'minority' that we humans invented. The argument goes, more or less, like this: use your reason and you will progress. You can't argue with that! Several of his ideas have stuck and accompanied me throughout my life because of their depth and authenticity. With our subject in mind, I quote from the book *Lectures on Ethics* (1775-1780):

> Animal nature has analogies to human nature, and by doing our duties to animals in respect of manifestations which correspond to manifestations of human nature,

we indirectly do our duty towards human-ity. Thus, if a dog has served his master long and faithfully, his service, analogous to human service, deserves reward, and when the dog has grown too old to serve, his master ought to keep him until he dies. Such action helps to support us in our duties towards human beings... If then any acts of animals are analogous to human acts and spring from the same principles, we have duties towards the animals because we thus cultivate the corresponding duties towards human beings.

Sovereign

Every cat is always able to be the most attractive
woman in the room.
Edward V. Lucas

Sovereign was beautiful in her way. She was an Angora cat with snow-white hair, emerald-green eyes and, unfortunately, FIV. Those who have some knowledge of cats know that this illness (full name: Feline Immunodeficiency Virus, also known as feline HIV) doesn't excessively shorten the cat's life. But Sovereign was also ten years old and, because of a tumour, had had the tips of her ears removed. She had spent almost all of her existence in the cattery, without cuddles and without a name. Like the others, I gave her one.

I needed a word able to convey the regality of her essence, the elegance of her movements, so that readers could understand that, despite the series of 'little problems' she had had, they were dealing with a wonderful being, inside and out.

It wasn't easy to condense all this into a name. I thought of many. At the time, I was teaching philosophy in a school and, between classes or during the afternoon break, I was looking around for inspiration. Actually, I was also trying to convince everybody at school to adopt a cat. One day, finally, I found the solution: 'Sovereign' undoubtedly conveyed a sense of regality. I was still a beginner and the description of the cat I initially wrote was still too brief. Only one person called, who was looking for a white cat for her elderly mother. She told me that she would only be able to come over in ten days time.

The problem was that the adverts weren't always published immediately upon being sent to the newspapers. Unfortunately, on this occasion, between the sending of the advert to the editorial office and its publication, a good week had passed during which Sovereign caught the mange. Even if it was a light form and immediately treated with drugs, ten days, the time we had before the lady came to see her, were not enough for her to look adoptable.

Luckily, more than two weeks went by. Sovereign was getting better and her hair, in the spots that were bald because of her illness, was growing back. I was delighted by the fortunate timing. Perhaps I would be able to give Sovereign a home after all. On the day of the appointment I went to the cattery two hours early. I had brought with me hair-cleaning spray, a comb and a blue bow to put on Sovereign's little collar. On her white hair, the result was remarkable: Sovereign looked irresistible.

Or so I thought.

The lady told me that Sovereign wasn't what she was looking for and that she would prefer an eight-month-old kitten instead. Besides the disappointment, I thought that to give an elderly lady a kitten was spiteful both to her and the cat. Not only do kittens need to be taken more often to the vet to be de-wormed, vaccinated and sterilised, they also need to be trained; they are hyperactive. A sweet and quiet cat, already well used to an apartment, seemed to me really much more appropriate. Nonetheless, to my great disappointment Sovereign stayed at the cattery.

The following day, a lady who wanted an adult cat called me on my mobile phone. I explained to her Sovereign's circumstances and she said: 'That's OK, it doesn't matter. Can you bring her?'

I said it was a pleasure for me to bring the cats to people's houses. It allowed me to check personally the environment in which they were going to live. I agreed with her that I would bring Sovereign there the next day at five thirty in the afternoon.

The following day, I put her in a carrier and off we went to the 'new home.'

The woman, who was from the Ukraine, was nursing an ill old lady and living together with her in a lovely house. To Sovereign, the garden probably appeared even lovelier. When the Ukrainian lady and the cat met, they liked each other immediately. Sovereign rubbed herself against the woman's calves receiving, in exchange, two heartfelt strokes. We went upstairs, the three of us following Sovereign on her first reconnaissance round. I asked her to fill in the form to record the adoption and left while Sovereign, like Bottoms Up, was lying on the bed.

Every time I was able to home a cat, I briefed the new owners on the animal's needs. For many of them it was their first experience with adopting a rescue cat. I had also written *The Little Guide to Cats*: a collection of practical tips – food, drink, tidiness, grass, exercise requirements – that I printed at home. After the adoption, I often called to see how the cat was adjusting and to be available for any advice that might be needed.

The happiness I felt was enormous. Afterwards, Sovereign's new owner gave me a call to let me know that the cat was doing well and was a good and pleasant companion for the ill old lady too.

I was so pleased.

A few months later, I happened to call the cattery and they told me: 'Did you know? They brought Sovereign back. About a week ago the lady came and told us that her employer had died. She has to go back to the Ukraine and can't look after the cat anymore.'

I felt as you are probably feeling now: very disappointed. I don't want to talk about animal sensitivity but, of course, we all know that they too perceive the difference between a welcoming and a hostile environment.

Sovereign wasn't leaving the cattery's garden. She hadn't eaten for a week and stayed outside, in the grass, separate from all the other cats. After all, having spent her entire life here, she had finally escaped and gotten to know cuddles, a bed and a garden of her own. Who could blame her?

I was so sorry for her that I immediately got down to work. In fact, having already put together several ads in the meantime, my powers of persuasion had got much stronger. I put so much effort into writing that advert that the very day it was published I received a huge number of phone calls (forty-three, to be precise). This was the advert:

Urgent Appeal for Sovereign

I have to launch an extremely urgent appeal for Sovereign, whose story I hope will touch someone's heart. The beautiful Sovereign is a sterilised, de-wormed cat, short ears, snow-white fur and beautiful green eyes, and she is now very unhappy. A cross-bred Turkish Angora with the thick (not long) hair typical of her breed, this poor cat has been living in a cattery for years. I did my best to have her adopted because she never really adjusted to community life. I was finally able to find her an appropriate home which allowed her to be reborn. The idyll lasted two months, but now Sovereign is back at the cattery because her new owner can't look after her anymore. Please, come and take her! She suffered a trauma from which she is not recovering: since she's come back, she doesn't eat and just lies still in the garden. She is fading away. Please, give a chance to this wonderful snow-white cat, who is elderly but very affectionate.

As always, I ended the ad with the two telephone numbers and the cattery's address. On the day of the publication, I happened to be travelling, attending to some errands. My mobile phone started ringing at seven thirty while I was on the train.

A young woman expressed her sadness about Sovereign: 'Poor thing, she must have felt awful, being abandoned like that!' She told me that she would come to take her in two hours. And so she did, Sovereign never came back to the cattery.

Piero Martinetti is an Italian twentieth century philosopher, but many don't know him. A fan of Kant, an expert on morality and respect for life, he wrote a book titled *Mercy for Animals*. You'll be deeply struck by the fact that some of his considerations still have such validity for us today. I was, when I read him:

> In the eyes of every dying animal is something human... surely a deeper understanding of animal life would induce, in any case, men to act towards these beings with a bit more of morality and mercy.

And, about his cat, Grisetto, the philosopher writes:

> He was just a poor cat: but this small being, whom I loved and who loved me, had a very important place in my life.

Perhaps it was because I thought like him that I did certain things. It was thoughts similar to his that urged me to do something when I was informed that Sovereign was exiling herself in the garden after being abandoned.

What would you have done?

Ying Yang

*Cats have an infallible understanding of
total concentration and get between you and it.*
Arthur Bridges

Elderly and 'unconventional' cats (i.e. those
without a paw, an eye, the tail, *etc.*) are, for obvious reasons, those who find a home less easily.
Ying Yang certainly looked 'unconventional.'
He had had one of his eyes removed due to an
infection. He permanently looked like he was
giving a wink but, overall, his face was agreeable, almost cute.

But there was another problem: he was easily scared, and hence shy. Such a cat is difficult
to place. Usually, people want an affectionate
cat, not one who runs away, even if only
because he's scared. The result is that the most
timorous and shy cats – who often become the
most affectionate in a welcoming environment
– stay and die in the cattery. Ying Yang, therefore, was a difficult case. He was an eight-
month-old kitten whom I had so named
because he was half white and half black. He

was the perfect balance of opposites, like the Oriental symbol. Furthermore, Ying Yang was at the cattery during a period when the cats urgently needing homes were numerous. The advert I wrote read like this:

> Ying Yang, a delightful eight-month-old kitten, already de-wormed and sterilised, is urgently looking for the patience and the sweetness of someone able to understand him because he is very scared. Christened with the name of the celebrated Oriental symbol linked to the balance of opposites because of the strength he showed despite the removal of one of his eyes, he could become a valuable friend to you.

The day the advert was published, nobody called. Two days later, a young voice on my mobile phone asked me: 'Is Ying Yang still available?' I explained the situation to her and she told me she would come and see him at the cattery.

She came back several times to visit Ying Yang. I learned, from her, that she had never had cats; she had to convince her mum and grandma. I told her, 'Consider that the cat must be able to move freely in the house so it's necessary that he is well liked by everybody.'

I told her that the adoption of an animal was a commitment that would last many years – she had to think about it very carefully. Very often people left cats they didn't want anymore at the cattery: sometimes these were cats who had been adopted as little as three years earlier. Initially I believed this was due to allergies – I know they can appear suddenly. But after the twenty-fifth person who used this excuse, I started to think there was something seriously wrong with the air in our town. I had never seen so many allergies all together.

One day I received a phone call: 'We all agree. So I am willing to fight this battle, but do you expect that Ying Yang will become sociable?' My answer was yes. He was only scared and it was a matter of patience. I would always remain available for advice.

She adopted him. An exchange of letters (well, text messages) followed. I asked for news and gave advice, and she reported on his antics. I suggested some tricks to conquer him, such as, 'Get close to him with food in your hand,' or some solutions to difficult situations like when Ying Yang took refuge under a bed or an armchair. After some time, the girl told me that she was starting to see some progress.

And boy was it progress.

At the cattery Ying Yang behaved like an eel. He slipped away as soon as he saw people coming in and was a cat difficult to love, especially for someone with little experience of the feline temperament. As I said though, this is a book that reports the wonders of reality; experiences of understanding, generosity and affection. Do not be too surprised, therefore, if I tell you that the first photo I received of Ying Yang pictured him seated on the window sill, belly up, being scratched by his owner!

The girl who adopted him told me that she was happy at having taken with her a cat that wasn't easy to re-home because of his 'little problem.' She was proud of having saved him from spending his entire life at the cattery.

And for this Ying Yang had rewarded her.

🐈

Animal gratitude is universally known. Every

one of us, I believe, has probably experienced it. We find it also in a fundamental work by the German philosopher Arthur Schopenhauer, an author not easy to describe in few words. One of his major works, *The World as Will and Representation* (1815), is a treatise of High Philosophy in which the following is put to the reader:

Animals too are capable of morality, affection, gratitude.

Itty-Bitty

Even overweight cats instinctively know the cardinal
rule: when fat, arrange yourself in slim poses.
John Weitz

When she arrived at the cattery, Itty-Bitty weighed 15 kilos. She belonged to the category of adult cats whose 'owner' (an ugly word, and inappropriate, since everybody knows you don't own a cat, but it's used here for the sake of brevity) had died and whose relatives didn't have any intention of looking after the cat or making the effort to find her a happy or, at least, a suitable home.

She was a bizarre, big cat – agreeable, but comical with her big belly, and strangely coloured: white underneath, grey-lilac on top. She was seven years old and had big yellow eyes and a pretty bad attitude. She hissed at anybody out of fear. She had spent all her life in an apartment with her lady-owner and had suddenly found herself in a strange, crowded room, without 'her' food… It must have seemed awful to her.

My advert had to convey all this. The readers and the people beyond had to know her situation and maybe someone would sympathise.

This is what I wrote:

Itty-Bitty's owner passed away. After seven years, she is alone and abandoned at the town's cattery. She is beautiful, nice and big (really big), with bi-colour white and lilac hair, large, sweet, yellow eyes and is not adjusting at all to her new environment.

Please, adopt her!

Unexpectedly, on the day of the publication, a girl called and told me: 'Hi. Sorry, I've never had cats, but the advert inspired me. Is Itty-Bitty still there?'

I explained to her the entire situation and, after the phone call and a day of appropriate reflection, the cat was adopted.

The new feline lover took home Itty-Bitty, but not the 'instructions for use.' I wasn't always able to print enough copies of my *Guide*.

A few days later, I talked to her by phone and she told me that the cat wasn't eating. When I heard what she had given her, I wasn't surprised at all.

What *did* surprise me was that, even after the

right feeding instructions, Itty-Bitty still wasn't eating.

There was something wrong.

With great difficulty I tracked down the telephone number of the dead lady's son, as it was he who had brought the cat to the cattery. Unthinkingly, he had forgotten to tell us about Itty-Bitty's peculiar gastronomical habits. This 'damsel' used to be fed only, guess what, rabbit's liver.

Those who abandon their animals in catteries or kennels (granted they should do anything they can to avoid it), should at least be wise enough to give all the information about any peculiarities in their animal's life.

When I heard about the liver, I understood why Itty-Bitty was refusing the food given to her and why she was so inexplicably big. She was bloated, not fat!

I explained the situation to the new adopter. The poor girl… She had never had cats and now she had to deal with Itty-Bitty's culinary penchant…

Nevertheless, she was very good at it, perhaps because she was strongly motivated. We kept in touch for a few more months and it was clear that a great friendship was born. Last time I saw her, Itty-Bitty was happy, affectionate and weighing 'only' nine kilos! Her new diet had made her more balanced, healthy and clean. Indeed, she was finally able to clean herself! All things considered, things had turned out well for Itty-Bitty.

But it's not always so in life. I don't want to go into matters like vivisection or the treatment of farm animals and of show animals, but it's a fact. Society, at least our industrialised one, believes that an animal life is worth less than a human one.

I think this is a quite complex subject that, certainly, cannot be dealt with appropriately here. Nonetheless, I will close this episode with a quotation from the celebrated philosopher Helmut Friedrik Kaplan. In a book about cats and philosophy, the name of this author, a vegetarian and advocate of animal rights, should be mentioned. This line is taken from *Animal Rights: The Philosophy of a Liberation Movement*:

> A living being's interest must not matter less simply because he belongs to a species different from yours.

Jerry

They told me that domestication of cats is very difficult.
It's not true. Mine domesticated me in a couple of days.
Bill Dana

I am sure that most people would agree that big tabbies are beautiful. It is perhaps because of their stripes, which evoke the seductive tiger's coat. But, unfortunately for Jerry, his most distinguishing feature was not his tiger stripes, but the braces on his teeth.

He had been brought to the cattery by his two owners and was still asleep from the anaesthesia he had received because of an operation on his mouth. Imagine what a pleasant awakening the cat must have had that day, finding himself in a cage, not at home, and with a piece of metal in his mouth that made chewing difficult.

And to think that his owners had the courage to say that they were very sorry… If they hadn't been, what would they have done to poor Jerry?

To make things worse, Jerry was also infected with FIV. It is actually quite common for an outdoor cat to be affected by this illness and its effects are easily exaggerated by its ominous acronym. I myself adopted a five-year-old cat with this 'mild affliction'. He is twelve now and still going strong which means that he has given me seven years of his life – filling it with his purrs.

This is why I chose not to write of the pretty and healthy kittens in the cattery. They were quickly adopted, without the need for publicity.

Rather, I invited people to reflect on the affection that adult cats can give.

It's true, as adults they had probably already settled into certain habits. But have you considered that these could be agreeable and, maybe, suit yours? Think about it. A cat who is already litter-trained, used to staying at home and who will fall in love with you and sleep on your lap because he has been abandoned and is missing his old owner's affection... These surely can only be advantages.

A cat lives, on average, thirteen or fourteen years, if not more. This means that if you adopt one who is already seven or eight years old, you can count on his company for the next six or seven years. Moreover, you would give a chance to a cat that, otherwise, would probably die, sad and alone, in a cattery.

There's no guarantee of course it will live for this long, but the same is true of a kitten and, after all, of a human being.

Maybe, the right thing for you is to adopt that very cat that 'talks' to you with his eyes, or with a little lick, or the purrs he offers you, even if he is seven years old.

Jerry didn't manage to talk anyone into adopting him, but fortunately a different opportunity presented itself.

Someone had called me for Nestor, a cat that had a bad cold and was therefore, in the vet's opinion, not adoptable for the moment. Jerry, on the other hand, was ready. His braces had finally been removed and he was able to chew perfectly. Unfortunately though, he wasn't adjusting at all to his new stressful environment in the cattery. He always stayed on the shelves inside and, at lunch time, he was extremely wary of all those tails surrounding the food bowl.

When I received the phone call for Nestor and arranged to take him to the new home, I hadn't been informed of the fact that he couldn't yet be adopted. As with Bottoms Up, when I arrived at the cattery, I had already made the adoption appointment with the new owner. The sadness I felt when they gave me the news about Nestor was deep. Days later this sadness would be increased when I saw him die of an infection.

I was also upset because I couldn't finalise the adoption, despite the availability of an adopter.

The best solution seemed to me to be to suggest Jerry to the new adopter. I saw him, as usual, on a shelf, beautiful and healthy: it was worth a try.

I arrived at the possible adopter's home with a cat that, instead of being black and white, was beige, brown and stripy.

Obviously, I had to be extremely clear, both in explaining what had occurred and in informing them about Jerry's history. The lady had a kind face. She listened to me and was a bit astonished, a bit doubtful, and a bit amused. She told me: 'Jerry is perfect. He is beautiful and affectionate.' Indeed, while I was explaining his story, the smart little cat had been working her, rubbing himself against her ankles and lifting her skirt's hem with the tip of his dark tail.

What an accomplishment! The adoption had gone well and Jerry, finally, looked like he was really comfortable.

I left, but after a week or so I had to go back to the cattery to settle some administrative details and decided to see whether I could later visit Jerry's new owner.

Whenever possible, I always go back to the adopter's home – both to check the kitten's health and to watch them revelling in their new-found happiness.

The last image I had of Jerry in the cattery was of him isolated on a shelf. When I arrived at his new home, I found him spread on a jumper between the two golden-yellow cushions of the sofa, loudly snoring.

Animals are able to give much, especially serenity and inspiration. It's not unusual to find them as muses in works of art or poems or, as in the case of pet-therapy, praised as exemplary conveyors of emotional healing.

Nonetheless, one can't say that we always return the favour. On this, Arthur Schopenhauer says in *Parerga and Paralipomena* (1851):

The total dedication to the present moment contributes so much to the delight we take in our domestic pets. They are the present moment personified, and in some respects they make us feel the value of every hour that is free from trouble and annoyance, which we, with our thoughts and preoccupations, mostly disregard. But man, that selfish and heartless creature, misuses this quality of the animal to be more content than we are with mere existence, and often works it to such an extent that he allows the animal absolutely nothing more than mere, bare life.

Mowgli

No amount of time can erase the memory of a good cat, and no amount of masking tape can ever remove his fur from your couch.
Leo Dworken

The streets were red and golden and full of lights.

Despite the cold winter there was a warm atmosphere, inviting and reassuring.

At the cattery however, things weren't quite so rosy. It happened that very day, Christmas Eve. At about seven pm, a lady called claiming she wanted to adopt a cat. I told her about Mowgli, a four-month-old kitten with big, lively eyes and a passion for cuddles, who had just arrived at the cattery.

She seemed interested, so we made an appointment for the following day, December the 25th. I was already enjoying the thought of finally taking little Mowgli away from that dismal place and putting him into the arms of his new owner.

The cattery was open every day, holidays

included, even if, in the latter case, the opening hours were limited to the morning. Christmas morning, at nine o'clock, I was there.

On arrival I stroked the ears of the unknowing cats, for whom Christmas was just a day like any other. But I knew that today might be a day to remember for little Mowgli. I had barely entered his room when he was in my arms, purring like a little engine, wriggling and warm.

When the bell rang, I opened the door and a lady came in. Mowgli appeared to like her. He made a little dance on his paws and wrapped his tail around his new friend's calves. He certainly knew how to play to the crowd.

I, on the other hand, was rather perplexed. The lady was explaining to me, in a pretty convoluted way, that she hadn't been able to buy a Christmas present for her son who had been asking for a cat for a very long time.

'But do *you* want a cat?' I asked her. She answered that a cat was an easier option than a dog or, rather, a more 'tolerable' one.

In just two minutes she had offered me the two main reasons why adoptions fail:

First: thinking of the animals as objects.
Second: not thinking carefully enough before adopting them.

'Tolerance' is not a sufficient basis for a fledgling relationship to be a success. It is necessary for everybody in the house not merely to assent but to really be open to cohabitation with a cat.

I know far too well how often tolerance is defeated by shredded curtains, hairy carpets and other feline trademarks; trademarks that are loved by cat people but are much less appealing to our fellow humans.

I did try to stress the responsibilities that come with adoption but, when it became clear that she wasn't listening, I simply refused to let her adopt him.

Of course, I wasn't thrilled at the idea of Mowgli remaining at the cattery. But I thought that it would be much worse to let him be taken away by someone who saw him as a thing.

I had seen it happen too many times before and knew what the outcome would very likely be. Moreover, the kitten had had a rather stormy past and I didn't want to take any risks.

The lady left, disappointed and outraged. And I was left feeling sorry for that little kitten but convinced of having acted in his best interests. However, this conviction was of little help when I had to look back into his big, liquid eyes.

I closed the door behind the lady with a lump in my throat.

It consoled me, however, that Mowgli could

count on his youth, sweetness and charm, which meant that the chances for him to be adopted were excellent. I knew that it was very unlikely that he would spend the rest of his life at the cattery.

What I couldn't know was that my every wish for him would be realised so quickly. Four days later little Mowgli was adopted by a wonderful couple.

When I saw him leaving the cattery in his carrier, I knew I had found the right adoption for him. It was an adoption that promised an entire lifetime of feline contentment: an adoption that was not just for Christmas.

Tabby

If man could be crossed with the cat, it would improve man but deteriorate the cat.
Mark Twain

Poor, sweet Tabby, the future must have looked pretty bleak from the inside of a rubbish bin.

It was summer. Her owner had packed to go on holiday, placed his suitcases in his car and, just before leaving, thrown his cat – along with her litter-box – into the rubbish bin.

You read that correctly: the rubbish bin.

This twit, however, had not taken into consideration that the law punishes cruelty to animals. Fortunately he had the decency to let a very shrewd lady, who was present at the scene, write down his number-plate.

Those who hurt animals sometimes forget that, wherever they are, someone could be watching them. Even during the darkest of nights or in the remotest of places, they may still discover that they will be held accountable for their actions. And this is what happened. You will be relieved to know that the idiot ended up paying for his crime.

But Tabby paid too… With her eye. While falling into the bin, she had seriously injured her right eye. When she arrived at the cattery, she was terrified. It took time before she regained her physical and psychological health.

For her, I wrote this advert:

Tabby – Saved from the Bin

Is there someone who wants this little kitten whose name is Tabby and whose eyes are the colour of amber? She is delightful and affectionate. In the picture, you can see her leaning against the wire of her cage. She was found in a closed rubbish bin! Someone had thrown her away with her bowl and her litter-tray. After the fall, an infection caused her to lose one of her eyes.

She is very cute, de-wormed and vaccinated, and clearly domesticated, and only needs someone who is willing to adopt and love her after such a negative experience. She looks like a little tiger!

Alongside this appeal I would also like to remind everyone that the law punishes, with imprisonment and large fines, those who abuse or abandon animals.

Recently, I had started to add pictures of the cats so that the readers could have a look at the subjects of my adverts. It proved, if I may say so, a stroke of genius.

As I said before, this book is about human generosity which, though often seeming in short order, does exist in abundance. Of this I had proof when the advert for Sovereign came out, and so it was with the one for Tabby. Lots and lots of people called both me and the cattery. All were deeply moved by the poor cat's story and willing to take care of her. Tabby was adopted by a lady who was already a happy owner of other cats. The latest news is that our friend is finally happy and peaceful.

❧

To close Tabby's story I want to add only these words taken from *The Rhetoric of Apology in Animal Rights: Some Points to Consider* (1994) by K. Davis:

> We are related to other animals through evolution. Our empathic judgments reflect this fact. It does not take special credentials to know that, for example, a hen confined in a wire cage is suffering, or to imagine what her feelings must be com-

pared with those of a hen ranging outside in the grass. We are told that humans are capable of knowing just about anything we want to know, except what it feels like to be one of our victims...

And these, taken from an article by R. Lockwood:

While not all those who abuse an animal will become serial killers, every serial killer has previously abused an animal.

Gorgeous

*A cat betters the wall of the garden in summer and
delights your heart in the cold winter.*
Judith Merkle Rilke

Some of you may think finding a home for a
young lady-kitten – one that is only a year old,
beautiful *and* Persian – should be a fairly easy
task.

Normally you would be utterly right, but
Gorgeous was the exception to the rule.

Before Gorgeous arrived at the cattery, she
had been segregated in a basement because the
child of her house was allergic to her. I can
never say it enough: before adopting an animal,
whatever the breed or the species, you must
carefully consider if you are really able to com-
mit to them until the end of their days. If so,
and you therefore decide to go through with the
adoption, it is certainly possible that an allergy
could suddenly develop, but you cannot keep the
animal in a basement for two months. You must
look responsibly for new accommodation. For a
start, you can turn to animal rights organisations

– present everywhere nowadays – which can offer you help and practical support.

In addition, there are catteries or kennels and various shelters that take on animals that don't have an owner.

Not only had Gorgeous been made miserable by her owners, she also came from a place that wasn't much happier – she had been bought in a shop. I don't want to cast any moral judgment on the purchase of a living being, but some shop keepers let the animals live in terrible conditions to move potential clients to pity and induce them to buy the animals. To purchase them, unfortunately, means to support a trade that is far from ethical.

This had been the story of Gorgeous, the little Persian. When she arrived at the cattery she was thin and dirty. She wasn't yet a year old and had already lived through all these terrible experiences. Despite all this, incredibly, Gorgeous still trusted human beings.

Each cat has a personality of their own, regardless of whether they are a purebred or not. I have to say though, that purebred cats manifest fairly marked character traits. For example, if you want a discreet, un-possessive, quiet cat, don't go for a Siamese. They are amazing, but very egocentric. I speak from experience. I've had two Siamese, both fantastic, but their personality is not to everyone's taste.

Persians are the opposite: they are all avatars of calm and tolerance. Well, almost all of them.

Therefore, as a purebred Persian, Gorgeous was very sweet – besides being good-looking. But I couldn't find an adopter, no matter how hard I tried.

Why? Because she was considered undesirable by the 'lovers of the breed'. And you can't imagine how many times people told me on the phone: 'She is already fairly grown up.' Grown up? At eleven months?

Actually, on this subject, I reached my lowest point when a seven-year-old, beautiful Persian – a real lion – arrived at the cattery. I wrote an advert for him, and a lady called me to ask about his age (I had already mentioned it in the ad). When I told her, she exclaimed: 'And what am I supposed to do with a seven year old cat?'

I wanted to say a lot of things, but none of them can be written here.

Anyway, Gorgeous had to find a home: she deserved it. The advert for her was like this:

Gorgeous is a young Persian cat, tortie-tabby. Very sweet, sterilised, de-wormed, vaccinated, domesticated. Her eyes are amber-yellow and her coat has golden and chocolate shades.

This advert, in a slightly longer version, worked as past ones had for the other cats.

I couldn't meet the couple who adopted her as I was working that morning. But it really was a joy for me to know that they would learn how much satisfaction and happiness you can give and receive when you adopt a rescue cat.

Once you have decided to share your sofa, bed, table (and whatever else) with a cat, then, regardless of your preferences, do go and take a look on the internet at the charities in your town that are caring for abandoned animals. You'll certainly find there, sooner or later, the one you are looking for.

Indeed, in these pages you have read about the alchemy that is created by an act of love: the one brought about by a cuddle, a smile, a loving gesture.

🐈

I think I have offered sufficient testimony (not only from philosophers but also from psychologists) as to the deep connection existing between animals and ourselves. But I hope you will allow me to stress this concept again through the words of Plutarch, a Greek philosopher who lived in the first century A.D. He was the author of works of great poignancy, still valid for us today, and in his *The Eating of Flesh, Discourse I* he wrote:

> Who could wrong a human being when he was himself so gently and humanely disposed toward non-human creatures?

Spitfire

It is difficult to obtain the friendship of a cat. It is a
wise, philosophical animal, one that does not place its
affections thoughtlessly.
Théophile Gautier

Spitfire was a beauty, a real panther. Entirely
black with yellow-green eyes, enlivened by that
typically feline sparkle – he was a prowling enig-
ma. He was among the 'difficult' ones at the cattery: elusive, wild, 'free'… In short, he was a true
cat. His body was fairly large, his neck powerful,
and he had a big, round head, perfect for resting
your hand on.

Because he wasn't laid back, I knew that we
had to work very hard on his adoption. He had
been brought to the cattery because he had
become an unwanted regular in somebody's garden.

To rescue an animal is both an easy and
responsible thing to do. I have always had much
respect for those who, when finding an animal
victim of a road accident, take it upon themselves to bring it to a cattery, a kennel or a shel-

ter. It's a gesture of great generosity and humanity. It can save the animal's life. Moreover, it is free.

However, even in this case, you have to be careful. For example, before taking a puppy away, it is better to see if its mum is nearby, otherwise you'll run the risk of disrupting breast-feeding.

Check if the sweet kitten who is rubbing himself against your legs already has an owner, even if he's not wearing a collar. The controversy on this last matter is never-ending. It is true that a collar doesn't suit the nature of cats, but it will tell you if they already have a family. You wouldn't believe how many cats arrive at the cattery because well-meaning people assume they are lost, only for the legitimate owners to appear, looking for them.

Spitfire had arrived at the shelter simply because he adored lingering in a garden belonging to a couple who didn't know how to get rid of him. Imagine... a free spirit, a 'roof-rider,' now forced into a pen too small to contain him and the other cats. The cattery, unfortunately, had only a certain number of rooms, so each one had multiple guests.

Spitfire couldn't understand why he and many others like him had been captured and were now locked in there. He was always at the window, looking at the green fields outside. It was heart-breaking.

I thought that it would be perfect for him to find a home with a garden.

This was the advert:

Urgent Appeal from the Cattery

Spitfire is the gorgeous cat in the picture. He has the powerful build and the shiny, thick hair typical of his Bombay breed. He has always been a free spirit, the embodiment of catness. He loves wandering around, and at the cattery he feels trapped, so depression has started to bring him down. He is extremely healthy, already sterilised, de-wormed, vaccinated, and litter trained. He keeps begging anybody passing by his cage to be taken away. He is sociable only with other cats.

Please, adopt him!

The first time the advert was published I didn't receive any phone calls. The second time, I had seven: *c'est la vie*.

I wasn't at the cattery when a young girl came with her mum to adopt him. They told me that the girl, cunningly, had brought with her a bag of dry food in order to seduce him... And she succeeded. I was also told that Spitfire's new home had a garden and a little basement from which he was free to sneak outside whenever he liked.

How important to you is respect for life? What's the meaning you give to it? To what do you extend it? On this matter, I'd like to suggest that you have a look at a book titled *Practical Ethics* (1979) by the contemporary Australian philosopher Peter Singer, one of the founders of the movement for the defense of animal rights. In it, you will read:

> ... having accepted the principle of equality as a sound moral basis for relations with others of our own species, we are also

committed to accepting it as a sound moral basis for relations with those outside our own species – the non-human animals.

Swami

I have seen more people healed by the company of a cat than by tons of drugs.
Enzo Jannacci

I've already written a little about the risks of letting your cat out without his collar. I understand the artificiality of it, but nonetheless, a collar is really helpful in tracking down cats, be they lost or stolen by passers by. When I started my voluntary job at the cattery, I had been told that lost cats were very rarely reunited with their owners. This was due, I guess, to the fact that people seldom think that their lost cat might have ended up in a cattery.

As always, the best way to start solving a problem is to make it known. As soon as I started writing ads for cats that had been found in the street, specifying date, place and appearance, reunions began.

We succeeded in reuniting twelve cats with their owners in this way. This means that twelve familes weren't left wondering in anguish where their feline friends might be and, above all, that twelve cats were not left behind at the cattery, at risk of spending the rest of their lives there. And all this thanks to just five lines in a newspaper.

A typical case is that of Swami. Obviously, I didn't know her real name when, one morning, she arrived at the cattery in a big box, eyes wide open out of fear, brought there by a Good Samaritan who had found her after she had been in an accident.

I still remember her, how loudly and for how long she meowed, poor thing...

Although she was very scared, she was clearly domesticated and very well cared for. Moreover, she was sterilised; therefore, she had to belong to someone. She had probably walked away from home and, after being hit by a car, hadn't been able to get back. She was a middle-sized kitten, tabby, with a nice little triangular muzzle. I added pictures to my adverts, especially those for found cats.

For Swami, I wrote this:

Cat Found in Our Neighbourhood

On the morning of the sixth of July the cat you can see in the photo was found in ... with her left back leg wounded. She is young, sterilised and sociable. Her coat is mostly tabby, with tortie-brown and copper shades.

It was useful to flag in the newspaper that a cat had

been found, but it was also possible that the owner wouldn't read it. Therefore, the adverts were always sent out two or three times.

In Swami's case I had to send it four times before the owner – to her, and my, great relief – contacted me and verified that we had the very cat she had lost.

It was a great feeling.

🐈

If it's true that the eyes are the mirror of the soul, Swami's eyes spoke volumes on the morning she arrived. You don't believe that cats have a soul? OK… Anyway, read what Schopenhauer had to say in *Parerga and Paralipomena* (1851):

> Only when people's minds are penetrated by the simple and unquestionable truth that animals are in substance and essence what we are will animals have rights and not be at the mercy of any gross rascal's mood and cruelty. Only then will quacks not be allowed to experiment, inflicting the most atrocious torments on innumerable animals, gratifying every ignorant or bizarre whim, as nowadays happens.

Cats and Newspapers

I have shared with you some of my most treasured memories. These were, however, by no means the only successes. Below I have given a further selection of the adverts from my time at the cattery that helped cats into the homes, and hearts, of new owners.

Daniel, Adoptable Sweetie

They found me in the street, abandoned, in despair.

At the cattery they gave me a name, Daniel. I have so many fine qualities. Here's the list:

I am affectionate and sweet, friendly and earnest, elegant and slender, a small, tender tabby. Castration is done and vaccination is soon to come.

I don't want to stay here, please come and adopt me!

Phillip the Cat

Black and white, really lovely, ready to be adopted. If you come during the day Phillip is here, waiting for you. He's only one year old, affectionate and well behaved, lively, cheerful and... castrated!

Marilyn for Adoption

Hello everyone, let me introduce myself. I am the starlet of the cattery, very nice and pretty, the queen of purrs. I am looking for a home and sweetness, strokes and cuddles; I never refuse any, I even chase them. I am only one year old, sterilised, sweet, cheerful and vaccinated. I ended up in the cattery and that's why you see me in the morning paper. Come on, adopt me... Think about it!

Well, then, I'll wait for you... Come over and pick me up.

Ask for Marilyn!

Appeal for Dakota and Casanova

Urgent appeal: gorgeous cats would like to go home.

Dakota is a fantastic and affectionate black and white cat (like Sylvester in the cartoon), already sterilised, vaccinated and de-wormed. If anybody wants her, she's packed and ready.

Casanova, unfortunately, is still waiting for an

adopter and he's becoming more and more depressed. He is a young, male, Brown Mackerel Tabby, with the typical stripes and a cream area on his muzzle and neck. He is very handsome, already sterilised, de-wormed and vaccinated. He is scared of strangers and he bends his ears in front of them. He looks rebellious, but he is only frightened.

Diocletian is Looking for a Home

Diocletian is the cross-bred Siamese, already castrated, de-wormed, and extremely affectionate and domesticated, that you can see in the photo. His case is unique: found almost dead on the street in the middle of March, it looked like he wasn't going to make it. Then, a miracle... I am appealing to animal lovers to give him the chance for a cuddle. He is not demanding and only needs someone to restore him to his past splendor.

Adopt Snuggles the Cat

Please, adopt Snuggles, a sweet, caramel-coloured cat.

Abandoned last summer, he managed by himself until the end of the season before he was brought to the cattery by a volunteer, who was looking after a cat colony, because he had bronchitis. Now he is healthy but depressed. His big, green eyes only sparkle when he is stroked. Please, come and see him.

Two Cattery Cats Looking for Adoption

Two kittens looking for homes.
The first one is a Norwegian lady-cat, named Princess because of her regality and beauty.

Liquorice, on the other hand, is not a pure-bred: she is black. Due to silly superstition, she has been left waiting at the cattery for months. The truth is that she is a gorgeous cat with wonderful, magnetic eyes.

Come and meet them.

Appeal for Nick the Beau and Sweet, Sweet Louise

Nick is a handsome Bombay cat. He is young, de-wormed, castrated, vaccinated, super-affectionate and looking for a home.

Louise is a delightful tortie cat. After a lifetime in an apartment, she was abandoned with her little sister, who has already been adopted. Therefore, she has spent Christmas alone at the cattery. Now the sweet Louise is very scared and would like a bit of love and peace. Is there anybody who wants to bring her the gift of a fresh start?

Please, Adopt Wimpy

If you had seen him when he arrived, he wasn't exactly 'petit.'

After his owner's death, this gorgeous, sweet, affectionate, sterilised cat, with a milk-white coat and yellow-orange eyes, couldn't find peace.

Wimpy is young (only three years old) and waiting to be adopted by someone special who can take care of him. He has cystitis (nothing serious!) which requires a bit of love and attention at home.

Don't leave him alone at the cattery.

Fasting Cissy is Urgently Looking for a Home

Cissy is the sweet and beautiful cat in the photo; she has yellow eyes and is two-three years old.

She was found abandoned with her litter and brought to the cattery. The kittens have been adopted, but she is still with us. Meanwhile, she has been sterilised, tested, and de-wormed; We know now that she is perfectly healthy. She is very good and affectionate but she doesn't accept the presence of other cats and is not eating much. She urgently needs a family to welcome her with love. Please, answer this appeal!

From Olympus to the Cattery...

Diana, Apollo and Zeus for adoption.

These kittens are good and a little shy, already litter trained. For each one of them a name has been chosen inspired by the Greek Gods...

Apollo: As graceful and elegant as the Greek god of music, he is a half white, half grey-tabby, two years old, de-wormed and sterilised.

Diana: Delightful silver-grey tabby kitten with a little, black, heart-shaped nose; like the Greek goddess, she is a skilled hunter of mosquitoes, small butterflies and anything else she can find. She is two years old, already de-wormed and sterilised.

Zeus: You see him in the photo with his sly expression... He is a grey and white tabby cat. He will make your life complete. He is two years old, de-wormed and sterilised.

Sweet Ginger is Looking for a Home

Ginger is a sweet adult female, tortoise-shell, sterilised and vaccinated.

After having spent seven years in a family, she has been brought to the cattery. It was a big shock for her. She doesn't trust humans anymore. She has been staying at the cattery for a long time but continues to remain isolated and eats very little. She needs a quiet family able to give her love and serenity so that she can recapture the taste for life that she has lost.

Please, at least come and meet her…

From Tibet with Love: Zen Is Looking for a Home

Zen is a really sweet cat, a meditative spirit: you can see him sitting at the highest spot in the room, just like philosophers when they are meditating. White and tabby, he is looking straight at the camera… He is two years old, de-wormed, sterilised and litter trained.

Come and meet him.

Urgent Appeal for Leone

Leone is a gorgeous black and white cat; he's about three years old and already sterilised. He has been the victim of an accident. He is all right now, but is not able to adjust to the cattery and refuses to leave his basket when it is important for him, after the surgery, to do some exercise.

We need someone to adopt him and take him away from here: he really doesn't want to stay at the cattery.

He is really super-sweet and very cuddly. His hair is longish and he's got a big tail.

Please, adopt him. Thank you, in advance.

Grumpus is Looking for a Home

Grumpus can neither understand nor come to terms with what has happened to her.

Adopted in … from the cattery, she was back in February of this year: the owner has abandoned home and cat.

She is a big, beautiful cat who easily fills a whole sofa seat. She is almost five years old, sterilised, de-wormed, vaccinated and litter trained.

Furry-tailed Asia and a Found Cat

Asia is a beautiful, aubergine coloured cat, full of charm, with a very furry tail to caress you, and middle-length, easy to brush hair on the rest of her body. Adopt her now… She is domesticated, sterilised and sociable.

Plus, I want to signal that the cat in the other photo has been found on … in … , at this address … , in the garden of a house.

Pure Devon Rex and Miuki for Adoption

At the cattery we have Sahara, a beautiful, pure

Devon Rex cat, already sterilised. She was found on the seventeenth of August in … . She is very sweet and affectionate.

Miuki is a gorgeous, black, young cat, already sterilised and vaccinated, very, very affectionate and urgently needs an adopter.

Also, a male (or female) adult, sterilised cat, very pretty and clearly domesticated, has been found in … on the sixteenth of August.

Two 'Moby Dick'-sized Cats for Adoption

The two big, adult cats in the photo, Bella and Calorie, are about five years old and have just arrived at the cattery because of their owner's death. They are both well domesticated: the grey and white one is shier, while the tri-colour is unbelievably cheeky. Both are 'Moby-sized,' sterilised, tested and de-wormed. They have always lived in an apartment and *cannot* remain at the cattery: please, adopt them.

The Beautiful Duchess is Waiting at the Cattery

You will certainly remember the beautiful Duchess in Walt Disney's *Aristocats*… An agreeable addition to the drawing-room, aristocratic and elegant.

If you come to the cattery, you will find her holding court.

Duchess is a blue and white Mackerel Tabby, already sterilised, de-wormed, vaccinated, domesticated and litter trained. She has been abandoned at the cattery and is not able to adjust. She asks nothing but to be adopted.

Please, Adopt Nina, Cross-bred Siamese

Here is the sad story of the gorgeous and heavenly Nina. A sweet and affectionate cross-bred Siamese with the typical blue eyes, she is healthy and has been brought to the cattery because her owner has moved to a care home. After years spent in an apartment, she is not adjusting to cattery life and urgently needs a new family. I won't tell you her age, I will only tell that she is *not* young. If you only wanted to give her a bit of serenity…

Answer this appeal! Thank you in advance.

Adopt the Blues Brothers

The Blues Brothers, black and white, one-year-old siblings, have been left at the cattery by their owner. He doesn't want them anymore and they, having known the apartment life, feel sad and lonely in this aseptic and crowded place. They are very sweet and sociable. Moreover, they love to be squeezed…

Please, answer this appeal for their adoption!

Adopt Sweet Kitten Chloe

There are no words to describe the super-sweet Chloe. She is only two and a half months and, as you can gather from the photo, she is incredibly cute.

I have named her Chloe, from the Greek word *chloe* meaning 'green and tender grass,' hoping this will be a good omen for her newborn life.

Apparently she is able to see only shadows, but this is not a problem, as cat lovers know, because cats are able to manage with their other senses; therefore, she leads an absolutely normal life.

Come soon and take her; she feels lost at the cattery.

Blessed and Santiago

I don't mind if a cat claims his own space. As long as his space is not the middle of my back at four in the morning.
Maynard Good Stoddard

After cats, dogs... It was inevitable that, loving animals and hoping to see as many of them as well placed as possible, I would end up writing adverts for dogs too. It was a natural progression.

The town's cattery was in front of the kennel. For obvious reasons it was not an ideal location. Many of the kittens who left the cattery ended up unexpectedly meeting some of the dogs walked by volunteers. Well, it was what it was.

The first time I went there was a Saturday afternoon.

Cat lovers who have only ever had cats find it difficult to get used to a canine presence. In place of purrs you get tail wagging. Instead of rubbing against you, the canine trots and runs around you. Instead of meow, woof. It's rather a major deal.

It took me a while to adjust, but nonetheless I felt sorry for them as well, seeing them in their cages and knowing about the awful experiences of abandonment and abuse that they had been subjected to.

This book is about cats and cannot allow too long a diversion on subjects of a different species, interesting and appreciable as they might be. But I have met thousands of dogs by whom I have been deeply touched. Therefore, once again, I urge you to look there for your pets. It will be a salve for your conscience and a blessing for the animals themselves. I came to know a very effective (and motivated) network of volunteers and witnessed incredible forms of dedication.

So, I started to add some dog stories to the cat ones. The number of dogs, compared to that of cats, was much higher, and the important thing was to inform everyone and invite them to come and visit our animal shelters. The rest would follow.

I wrote about a kennel where dogs were being kept in concentration-camp like cages, the existence of which I had been informed of by some volunteers, and, to my great satisfaction, the advert led to adoptions. Most of the time, however, I wrote about the furry guests of my town's two kennels who were cared for devotedly, but were looking for homes anyway.

I will include here only one advert:

Blessed and Santiago
Appeal for a Cat and a Dog

Blessed, aka Benny, is the super-nice and young kitten in the photo. When you look at her, she conquers you: little, sweet eyes, and a tender, small muzzle and full of love. She would suit someone who likes dynamic and playful cats.

At the kennel on... Street, Santiago has been waiting for a long time. He is a sweet, black and white hound who, adopted once before, lived happily with his owners for eight years until they moved and brought him back to the shelter.

Just imagine how discouraged and abandoned he must have felt. Come and meet him: he will win your heart.

As I said, for many dogs the adverts worked. But not for Santiago, unfortunately. What really moved me was that when it was time for him to have his picture taken, he struck a pose on his own initiative; it almost looked like he knew the reason for what we were doing... It was very touching.

For this canine episode, and others I haven't mentioned, I will 'steal' from Mark Twain's indomitable wit a reflection that says a lot:

> Heaven goes by favour; if it went by merit, you would stay out and your dog would go in.

Little Dove

A cat-less writer is almost inconceivable. It's a perverse taste, really, since it would be easier to write with a herd of buffalo in the room than a cat. They make nests in the notes and bite the end of the pen and walk on the typewriter keys.
Barbara Holland

It is with her that I want to end my book because, somehow, it's with her that everything began. Little Dove was part of the group of cats I first met when I arrived at the cattery.

She wasn't beautiful, but she was special. I can't say why... Maybe because of her sweet nature, or those small black spots on her milk-white coat. Maybe for her eyes or, maybe, for her story. She had been brought to the cattery some time earlier, aged ten, because of the death of her owner. This cat had always lived in an apartment. Who knows what she must have felt – at an age comparable to the human seventies – in a cold, aseptic place, with no laps to sit on and no hands to slip under. I often wondered what she was thinking.

It was heartbreaking. She was always to be found in the corner of her room, lying on the floor. The advert for her was one of the first I wrote. It was one of the most heartfelt, and I distributed copies of it everywhere: professional groomers' boards, vets, pet shops... Just about everywhere. I just wanted this poor, sweet cat to have a bit of peace again.

It had worked for many other kittens and would work for many more, but, for Little Dove, it didn't.

I asked for her to be visited by a vet because she had been moving very little. They told me it was pneumonia.

Little Dove was old and maybe, having lost any hope of leaving the cattery, she had renounced life.

The following Monday morning I was informed of her death and, when I asked where she was, they pointed at a black rubbish bag. It was there, then, that her hopes and life had ended up.

Forgive me for choosing to end with her story, but I hope you will understand my reasons. If someone had written an advert for Little Dove when she arrived at the cattery, she might have had a few more happy years and a peaceful end. So I hope that at least some of you will decide to write a few adverts for the cats in your town's shelters so that there won't be any more stories like that of Little Dove...

I won't quote the advert I wrote for her: it didn't help and she died without being placed.

But, as I told you at the beginning of this book, my aim is to warm your heart in the hope that you, too, one day, will decide to lend a hand and warm other people's hearts in turn. Unless, that is, you are already doing it.

🐈

Being very fond of Piero Martinetti, it's with his words that I want to end. He wrote them for his cat:

I will always remember her small, innocent

muzzle, her simple and good eyes that always looked at me with ingenuous wonder when I looked at her with tenderness.

And, in his *Mercy for Animals* (1999):

Why does the sight of this small, dear being, forever still, move and grieve me deeply in my soul? In her death I cry the great death of all, of love, of hope, of the dearest ties. In this bitter loss I feel the irreparable bitterness of all losses, the desperate and vain revolt against fate that ends, one after the other around us, all the things that are most intensely ours, everything that is part of us.

Afterword

Thank you for reading my book. If you wish to contact me to express your thoughts and opinions or to find out more information about animals, you can reach me at the following e mail address: filosofia_gatti@hotmail.it.

I will be happy to hear from you!

Appendices

Appendix I

Cats and Names

As I said, healthy kittens are easy to place: who wouldn't be won over by a cute little creature, looking at you with sweet, huge eyes?

In these cases, my assistance wasn't necessary, unlike for those cats at risk, because of their age or other 'little' problems, of remaining and dying at the cattery. Just like Little Dove.

Having limited space, I had to select only a few stories for this book. Nonetheless, not wanting to omit any of my furry friends (each one of them, in fact, has inspired me) I have decided to name all the cats I have known, christened and sponsored.

You can use your imagination, if you wish, and try to picture them, helping me to keep alive their sweet memories (remember that I chose the name according to the cats' personalities).

The following order is not alphabetical but chronological.

Little Dove
Bottoms Up
Mouse
Caesar
Moo
Sovereign
Ying Yang
Itty-Bitty
Jerry
Tabby
Gorgeous
Spitfire
Dakota
Billy
Casanova
Chief
Red
Susie
Darling
Crumpet
Bella and Calorie
Herby
Matisse
Cyrus
Mimi
Silver Moon
Lucy
Lola
Patch
Lady
Arthur
Foggy

Sandy
Athos, Aramis and
Porthos
Princess
Liquorice
Bon-bon
Mocha
Chub-chub
Paprika
Big Potato
Cecilia
Hope
Angel
Matty
Scrappy
Paris
Gaudi
Bistrot
Milo
Sahara
Quicksilver
Strawberry
Marie-Charlotte
Tiger
Little Saint
Nick
Thelma and Louise
Wimpy
Ralph and Marcello
Diva
Garfield and Pin Pin
Swami

Appendix II

Garfield and Pin Pin
From Paris with Love

A cat would never sleep on a mediocre book.
(Harold Weiss)

Sometimes, events occur in your life that are so unexpected that you can't help but wonder: 'Is this really happening to me?' That's what I thought when I was offered the opportunity to go and live in Paris.

Suddenly, I found myself enveloped in the atmosphere of the Ville Lumière, surrounded by the Seine, exhilarated by the colours of Notre Dame's stained glass windows. I was swept up in a whirlwind of lights, smells and music. Listen to the song by Jacques Dutronc, *Il est 5 heures, Paris s'éveille…* ('It's five o'clock, Paris is waking up…') and it'll help you to understand what I mean.

If you have never been to this extraordinary city, then go, even if only for one night. Whatever your job or your interests, in Paris you'll find something to captivate you.

A tip: visit the Louvre in the evening, when the pyramid (yes, the one in *The Da Vinci Code*) is lit up. Together with the moon, it creates a surreal contrast with the austerity of the court of the former Royal Palace.

But let's not digress... We are here to talk about cats.

Well, I found evidence of their presence all over the French capital.

My first encounter was on a street in the nearby Latin Quarter. This street, called *Rue du chat qui pêche*, is in the artists' area; there are always cats where there is creativity. Literally, the name of this road means 'the fishing cat road.' Nothing unusual in that; a cat that fishes doesn't seem like a strange idea at all. But in French, as well as in Italian, *pêcher* (to fish) also means to find out. So when you put two and two together you get a more interesting interpretation, one that speaks to the feline nature: cats are able to seek out, to root out uncommon things.

I found a second cat on a bag: it was the *Chat Noir*. This bag – as with thousands of other items you will notice if you stroll the streets of Paris – had printed on it the image of a big, black cat, symbol of the celebrated cabaret theatre situated at the foot of Montmartre Hill. At the end of the nineteenth century, Rodolphe Salis decided to open a café and called it *The*

Chat Noir, after a black cat found abandoned in the construction site. This café became one of the cult meeting places in Paris during the *Belle Époque*, in spite of those who think that black cats are bad luck. Needless to say, Monsieur Salis loved cats: he was an artist.

I spotted other cats painted on the highest corners of some buildings: big, yellow cats, with a sly sneer on their face. They are also known as *perchés* because they decorate these high corners that are very difficult to reach. Because the artist remains anonymous, there are several theories about his possible identity. The one thing we can be sure of is that he must be extremely fit: it's no mean feat to decorate the seventh floor of a building without any scaffolding.

I met another cat during a stroll, on a summer afternoon, near the Pantheon. Maybe it was just by chance that I met such a cat – soon you will know more about him – next to the place where Foucault's Pendulum hangs (well, not the original one, but a copy that re-enacts his experiment); a place that extended hospitality to some of the greatest philosophers of the eighteenth century: Rousseau, Voltaire, Condorcet. Just in front of Condorcet's former home, not far from the Pantheon, I stopped. It was a moment of meditation. I had studied Condorcet for one of my university examinations. Full name: Jean-

Antoine-Nicolas Caritat, Marquis of Condorcet, great philosopher of the Enlightenment, by whom I had read the work titled: *Sketch for a Historical Picture of the Progress of the Human Spirit.*

In simple terms, it is a book about the progress of humanity; the full attainment of which is represented by the overcoming of inequalities between nations, by the extension of equality to individuals and peoples and, eventually, by the improvement of human nature itself. With this in mind, how could one not stop in front of his home?

It was a bit further, on the street corner, that the encounter took place. A long – *very* long – blond cat yawned at me from the window of an antique dolls shop. He was lying on a red-purple tapestry between the glass and an armchair. What a Machiavellian mind that shop owner must possess... What better window-dressing than a big cat that stretches his paw when you call him? And Parisians know it well. It is in fact rather common to see cats in the shop windows.

It so happened that I came to know of the existence of *L'École du Chat*, the Cat School. There are several of these schools, and they extend hospitality to abandoned cats. These houses are often made available by volunteers who look after the cats until they are adopted. Their inspiring work struck a chord with me.

Despite the fact that I had left home, (and I knew I would stay away for a few years) I didn't want to leave 'my' cats at the cattery. Thankfully the internet would allow me to stay informed and to write adverts for them.

Garfield and Pin Pin's story belongs to these Parisian times… It is one of the most difficult to tell because it is one of the most delicate. The story of these two cats entwines in an extraordinary way with that of their owner, who would have done anything to hold onto them. B., – as I will call him from now on – alone and affected by an unforgiving illness, had adopted the gingery Garfield and, subsequently, the tabby Pin Pin.

After some time, he was admitted to the hospital. Despite his illness, he had looked for someone trustworthy to care for the cats while he was away and had found a neighbour willing to help him.

It was during his absence that one of B.'s relatives arrived at the cattery and abandoned the two cats there, unbeknown to B.

Maybe you are wondering why they did this. I do not know. Both Garfield and Pin Pin reacted badly: refusal of food, loss of hair. At the time, I met a few difficulties in re-homing them, but nothing exceptional. I succeeded, but had to place them separately. Garfield was adopted by an English family, Pin Pin by a family who already had another cat. About three weeks later, B. went back home and was devastated by the absence of his friends. He called the cattery and, crying desperately, demanded to have 'his darlings' back.

Normally, cats cannot be given back: those who relinquish them lose any rights. Obviously this time the situation was different, given that the two kittens had been abandoned without their owner knowing it. In the end, we made an exception. I took it upon myself to retrieve Garfield and Pin Pin from their families – who were rather unhappy at the idea of losing their cats – and bring them back to the young man. It was also a way to get to know his situation better. When I arrived, the cats were happy and the man grateful: he told me how much they meant to him and thanked me profusely.

Around two years later the cats were abandoned for the second time at the cattery. One morning a man, very upset, came over with both of them in a cage and told us: 'B. died and I cannot look after his cats.'

This sent a cold chill down my spine. However I was pleasantly surprised by the fact that, despite his severe illness, B. had continued to take care of the cats very well: his two furry friends were very beautiful and rather plump. He had really loved them.

The two cats seemed to be coping reasonably well, as long as they remained together in a room of their own. But when Pin Pin was adopted, Garfield had to move in with the other cats and that was the beginning of the end: refusal of food and dull, questioning eyes. He hadn't been adopted because he was FIV positive.

How could I let this story end in this way, knowing of the odyssey the two cats had already been through and knowing how much they had meant to B.? The advert I wrote, and sent everywhere, was this:

Perhaps some of you read my advert, published over the last few days, about the two cats, Garfield and Pin Pin. Luckily, Pin Pin has been adopted. But Garfield, by himself, is not making it. He is handsome, gingery with green eyes, used to an apartment, litter trained and really sweet, besides being super affectionate. He has turned out to be FIV positive, but allow me to remind you that he is *not* contagious for people or dogs and does *not* require medical assistance. It's rather a weakening of his immune system and he can easily live until twelve years old or more! Hence, we are dealing with an absolutely normal cat, as you can see from the picture. Therefore, if among you or your acquaintances there is someone willing to adopt him, besides gaining a fantastic companion, it would be a wonderful gesture. Please, think about it and do not condemn him without having met him in person. Pay him a little visit, just to get to know him… Thank you.

It was a wonderful lady, knowledgeable about cats, who called: she already had a female kitten – not infected with the virus – and she knew that FIV is an illness transmissible only sexually or during possible fights. This wasn't a possibility for either of the cats, so this helpful and trustworthy lady came over the following Saturday and adopted Garfield.

She was a special person, capable of looking beyond the obvious, as many other people I had met thanks to the adoptions have been, and, maybe, as you yourself are.

I soon received a picture from her and, one month later, a second one: Garfield was sleeping in a fruit case, a sly muzzle on a body shaped like a plump number eight.

The story of Garfield and Pin Pin probably doesn't need any comments or reflections, only the joy of the happy ending. Nonetheless, given that we are talking of animals and philosophy, I'd like to explore a few aspects further.

You certainly know that respect for life in general – not only for humans – has been supported for centuries by philosophers and religions. Buddha Gautama (circa 563-486 B.C.), in one of his five *Sutra Agame* of the *Pali Canon*, the *Majjhima-nikaya* (middle-length discourses), wrote:

> I was always mindful in stepping forwards and stepping backwards. I was full of pity even for the beings in a drop of water; thus, let me not hurt the tiny creatures in the crevices of the ground.

More or less in the same period of time, the Greek Philosopher Pythagoras (circa 560-480 B.C.) wrote:

> Anything man does to animals will be paid back with the same coin.

Tiruvalluvar, an Indian poet who was born between 100 and 800 A.D., wrote a book titled *Thirukkural* in which we find these words:

Those whose heart is inclined to compassion will never be dragged to the dark, painful hell. The evil karma, feared by the soul, will not afflict the merciful one who adopts and protects any life.

We find similar considerations in contemporary Western thought.

Albert Schweitzer, a theologian and medical doctor (and much more) who lived between the nineteenth and the twentieth centuries, wrote:

Ethics, in the widest meaning of the word, is a sense of responsibility extended to everything that has life.

Norberto Bobbio, a twentieth-century Italian philosopher, in his book *Left and Right,* said on this same matter:

Never as in our age have class, race, sex, the three principal sources of inequality, been questioned. The gradual recognition of equality between men and women, first in the little society of family, then in the larger civil and political society, is one of the most definite signs of the irreversible progress of human beings towards equality. And what about the new attitude towards animals? Ever more frequent and extensive are debates regarding the rightness of hunting, the limits of vivisection, the protection of endangered animal species, vegetarianism. What are they if not first signs of a possible extension of the principle of equality beyond even the frontiers of the human, an extension based on the awareness of the fact that animals are our equals, at least in that they can feel pain?

It is clear that to understand the sense of this historical movement it is necessary to raise our eyes from everyday skirmishes and look higher and further.

Giovanni Martinetti, in his *Equality in Suffering*, claims:

Modern man suffers from the worst kind of heart diseases: the inability to love with his heart. Many think that to love with one's heart, and to love animals too, is merely emotional sentimentalism. It is, instead, a form of moral sanity and a rationality which is deeper than the selfish one.

There are many more testimonies, but those

reported above already show that respect for animals is not just merely the preserve of fanatics.

Appendix III

Cats and Poets

Have you ever heard of Tom Quartz? Mark Twain writes about him in *Dick Baker's Cat*. And what about *The Cat Who Walked by Himself* by Rudyard Kipling? Or the cat from Havana in *White and Black Dynasties* by Theophile Gautier?

And don't forget Émile Zola, James Herriot, Margaret Bonham and many others who all wanted to write about cats.

Literature has paid much homage to cats. You have read some of these tributes under the titles of the episodes I have recounted. You'll find others in the following pages. Each one of them reaffirms the importance of knowing a cat...

The Cat from *Bestiary* by Guillaume Apollinaire

In my house I want:
A reasonable woman,
A cat passing among the books
And friends in every season
Whom I cannot live without.

The Cat by Giovanni Pascoli

There was a cat, very trite, and it wasn't
Anybody's, and, old, it had its kitten.
Now, one night, (up the chimney
the storm gushed and roared)

The sound of a prayer drew me to the door
And I saw her and her kit next to her.
She sweetly pushed the wretched thing
Between my feet and disappeared into the black night.

What a black night, full of pain!
Tears and sobs and mad laughter and dark
Howls brought in from the desert wind.

And the rain was falling, huge roars
Whipping the house walls and rattling the windows.
The little one was purring, contented.

The Cats Will Know by Cesare Pavese

Rain will fall again
on your smooth pavement,
a light rain like
a breath or a step.
The breeze and the dawn
will flourish again
when you return,
as if beneath your step.
Between flowers and sills
the cats will know.
There will be other days,
there will be other voices.
You will smile alone.

The cats will know.
You will hear words
old and spent and useless
like costumes left over
from yesterday's parties.
You too will make gestures.
You'll answer with words –
face of springtime,
you too will make gestures.
The cats will know,
face of springtime;
and the light rain
and the hyacinth dawn
that wrench the heart of him
who hopes no more for you –
they are the sad smile
you smile by yourself.
There will be other days,
other voices and renewals.
Face of springtime,
we will suffer at daybreak.

For I Will Consider My Cat Jeoffry
from *Jubilate Agno* by Christopher Smart

Christopher Smart's devotion to cats is extraordinary. He is an eighteenth-century, English poet who was confined in a mental hospital for many years. The above mentioned work is dedicated to his cat, Jeoffry, who "saved" him – inspiring him and leading his mind beyond the gloomy atmosphere of the place in which he was kept.

The following is a sublime and upsetting

poem that seemed to me the best way to end this varied ensemble of literary tributes to cats. You will sense in it the presence of the cat just like you do at night, when you can't see him, but you can feel his steps.

For I will consider my Cat Jeoffry.
For he is the servant of the Living God duly and daily
    serving him.
For at the first glance of the glory of God in the East
    he worships in his way.
For this is done by wreathing his body seven times
    round with elegant quickness.
For then he leaps up to catch the musk, which is the
    blessing of God upon his prayer.
For he rolls upon prank to work it in.
For having done duty and received blessing he begins
    to consider himself.

For this he performs in ten degrees.
For first he looks upon his forepaws to see if they are
    clean.
For secondly he kicks up behind to clear away there.
For thirdly he works it upon stretch with the forepaws
    extended.
For fourthly he sharpens his paws by wood.
For fifthly he washes himself.
For sixthly he rolls upon wash.
For seventhly he fleas himself, that he may not be
    interrupted upon the beat.
For eighthly he rubs himself against a post.
For ninthly he looks up for his instructions.
For tenthly he goes in quest of food.
For having consider'd God and himself he will
    consider his neighbour.

For if he meets another cat he will kiss her in
kindness.

For when he takes his prey he plays with it to give it a
chance.

For one mouse in seven escapes by his dallying.

For when his day's work is done his business more
properly begins.

For he keeps the Lord's watch in the night against the
adversary.

For he counteracts the powers of darkness by his
electrical skin and glaring eyes.

For he counteracts the Devil, who is death, by
brisking about the life.

For in his morning orisons he loves the sun and the
sun loves him.

For he is of the tribe of Tiger.

For the Cherub Cat is a term of the Angel Tiger.

For he has the subtlety and hissing of a serpent,
which in goodness he suppresses.

For he will not do destruction, if he is well-fed,
neither will he spit without provocation.

For he purrs in thankfulness, when God tells him he's
a good Cat.

For he is an instrument for the children to learn
benevolence upon.

For every house is incomplete without him and a
blessing is lacking in the spirit.

For the Lord commanded Moses concerning the cats
at the departure of the Children of Israel from
Egypt.

For every family had one cat at least in the bag.

For the English Cats are the best in Europe.

For he is the cleanest in the use of his forepaws of
any quadruped.

For the dexterity of his defence is an instance of the
love of God to him exceedingly.

For he is the quickest to his mark of any creature.

For he is tenacious of his point.
For he is a mixture of gravity and waggery.
For he knows that God is his Saviour.
For there is nothing sweeter than his peace when at
  rest.
For there is nothing brisker than his life when in
  motion.
For he is of the Lord's poor and so indeed is he
  called by benevolence perpetually-Poor Jeoffry!
  Poor Jeoffry! The rat has bit thy throat.
For I bless the name of the Lord Jesus that Jeoffry is
  better.
For the divine spirit comes about his body to sustain
  it in complete cat.
For his tongue is exceeding pure so that it has in
  purity what it wants in music.
For he is docile and can learn certain things.
For he can set up with gravity which is patience upon
  approbation.
For he can fetch and carry, which is patience in
  employment.
For he can jump over a stick which is patience upon
  proof positive.
For he can spraggle upon waggle at the word of
  command.
For he can jump from an eminence into his master's
  bosom.
For he can catch the cork and toss it again.
For he is hated by the hypocrite and miser.
For the former is afraid of detection.

For the latter refuses the charge.
For he camels his back to bear the first notion of
  business.
For he is good to think on, if a man would express
  himself neatly.
For he made a great figure in Egypt for his signal
  services.

For he killed the Ichneumon-rat very pernicious by land.

For his ears are so acute that they sting again.

For from this proceeds the passing quickness of his attention.

For by stroking of him I have found out electricity.

For I perceived God's light about him both wax and fire.

For the Electrical fire is the spiritual substance, which God sends from heaven to sustain the bodies both of man and beast.

For God has blessed him in the variety of his movements,

For, tho he cannot fly, he is an excellent clamberer.

For his motions upon the face of the earth are more than any other quadruped.

For he can tread to all the measures upon the music.

For he can swim for life.

For he can creep.

Appendix IV

Pawsabilities for Cat Rescuers

1: Seek out your nearest cat home

British Catteries: An Independent Directory of British Catteries – britishcatteries.co.uk

Animal Samaritans, Kent
Battersea Dogs and Cats Home
Cat and Kitten Rescue, Borehamwood
  Cats Protection have branches all over the UK - (London: Bexley & Dartford, Croydon, Greenwich, Eltham, Sidcup, District, Hendon, Finchley & Mill Hill, Hillingdon, Lea Valley; Manchester: Trafford, Atherton, Wiggan & Metro Areas, Bolton and Radcliffe, Rochdale; Oxford: Oxford, Cherwell; Berkshire: Bracknell & Wokingham, Maidenhead & Slough, Newbury, Reading; Essex: Basildon, Brentwood & District, Chelmsford & District, Colne Valley, Harlow, Epping Forest & District, Hornchurch & District, Rayleigh, Castle Point & District, Romford & District, Southend & District; Kent: Bromley, Dartford, Maidstone, Sittingbourne, Swale, Tenterden, Tunbridge Wells, Canterbury, Folkestone; Hampshire: Winchester & District, Fareham & Waterlooville, Andover & District, Basingstoke & District, Farnham & Wey Valley, Gosport Town, Portsmouth, Southampton; Sussex:

Hailsham, Haywards Heath, Horsham, Crawley, Worthing, Hastings, Lewes; Wiltshire: Swindon, Salisbury, Wootton Bassett & District, Frome; Somerset and Bristol: Glastonbury & Wells, Minehead, Taunton, Yeovil, Weston-super-mare; East and West Midlands: Birmingham, Stourbridge & District, Cramar, Warwick, Avon, Rugby, Coventry, Evesham; Yorkshire: York, Scunthorpe & District, Leeds, Lancashire, Mansfield; Scotland: Perth, Glasgow, Dundee, South Ayrshire, Arbroath & Carnoustie, Aberdeen, North Ayrshire, South Ayrshire, Cumnock & Doon Valley)

Mayhew Animal Home, Brent
National Animal Welfare Trust
Wood Green Animal Shelter
Tameside Animal Shelter, Hyde
Sunshine Cat Rescue, Oxfordshire
The Blue Cross Lewknor Adoption Centre, Oxon
Battersea at Old Windsor, Berkshire
Thames Valley Animal Welfare
Cat Rescue Essex
Chestnut Cat Sanctuary, Essex
Colchester Cat Rescue
The Scratching Post, Enfield
Romney House Cat Rescue, Downe
Orpington Cat Rescue
Medway Cat Trust, Gillingham
Cats in Crisis, Thanet
Lymington Cat and Kitten Rescue
As Soon as Possible Cat Rescue
Happycats Rescue
Paws and Claws Animal Rescue, Sayers Common
Lost Cats Brighton
Cat Rescue, Wiltshire
Cats Action Trust, Wiltshire
St Giles Kennels and Cattery, Somerset
Cats Action Trust, Somerset
Yorkshire Cat Rescue

Cats Protection League, Belfast

2: Politely ask if you can look around (call or email ahead so that you are can be certain the busy cattery staff will have time for you!)

3: Investigate volunteering opportunities. Think about how much time you're realistically willing to devote, and go for it!

There are hands-on welfare roles, such as cat carer, home visitor, cat fosterer, lost and found cats volunteer, and rehoming volunteer
    Other roles include secretary, treasurer, fundraiser, administration volunteer, helpline phone and/or email volunteer, newsletter editor, publicity volunteer, and recruitment volunteer...all of which are vitally important to any charity's sustained success

4: Whatever your role, get to know each of the cats for who they are. If they don't have names, spend a little time with the cats and pick the one that most suits them. Imagine how they could be described to bring out their own unique personality in an advertisement and then pick your name.